Goats and Sheep

by Suzannah Ditchburn

T0355244

Say the sounds.

/oa/	oa *as in goat*
/short oo/	–oo *as in cook*
/long oo/	oo *as in spoon*

Blend the sounds to read the words.

woolly	soap	groom
goat	good	food

Goats

strong teeth

tail

coat

hoof

Sheep

woolly tail

coat

hoof

Goat habits

Goats can jump on rocks.

This goat is good on its feet!

A goat sleeps on its tummy.
It needs a dry bed.

Sheep habits

Sheep are happy in flocks.

Sheep sleep lightly. They might get a fright in the night.

Keeping goats

goat food

They are hungry goats!

The coat needs a brush.

I am grooming its coat.

Keeping sheep

This sheep has thick wool.
It needs cutting.

Food and drink from goats

We get lots of good things from goats.

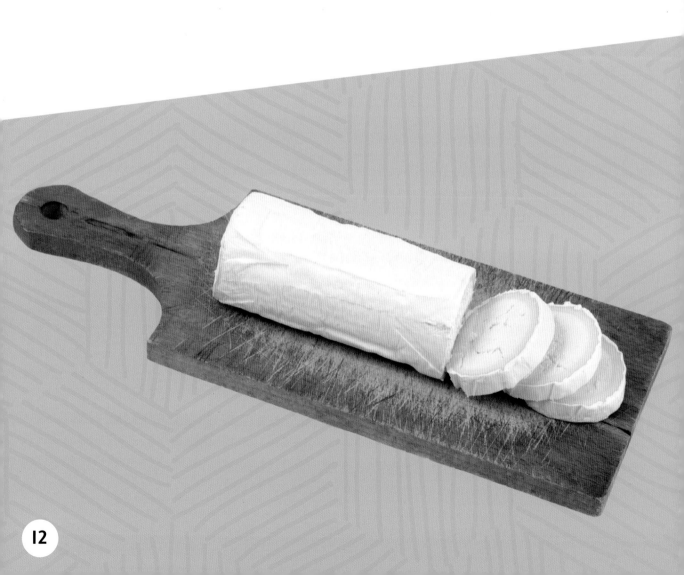

We can drink goat's milk.
We can get soap from goat's
milk, too.

a jug of milk

soap

Things we get from sheep

We get lots of wool from sheep.

wool rug

woollen coat

woolly hat

We get good food from sheep, too.

milk

feta

Feta is good on toast!

Talk together

1. Which animal needs its coat cutting?

2. How and where do goats like to sleep?

3. Which of these things do we get from sheep?